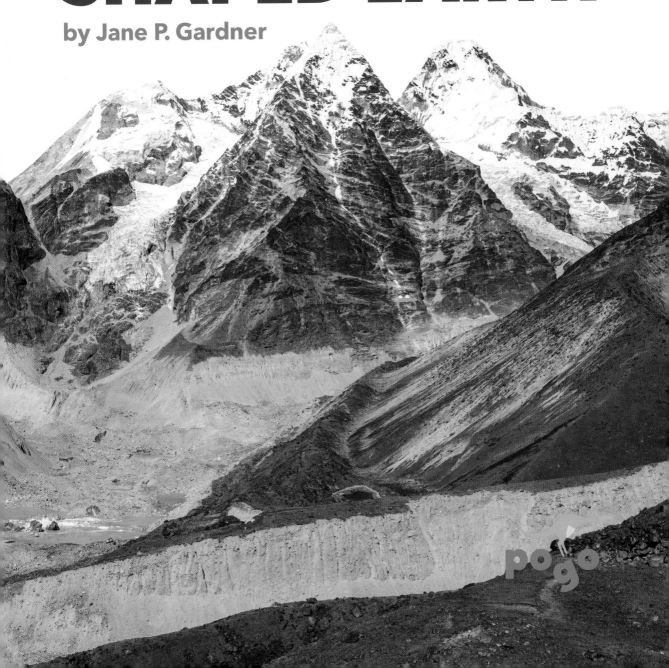

EARTH SHAPERS
HOW TECTONIC PLATES
SHAPED EARTH

by Jane P. Gardner

pogo

Ideas for Parents and Teachers

Pogo Books let children practice reading informational text while introducing them to nonfiction features such as headings, labels, sidebars, maps, and diagrams, as well as a table of contents, glossary, and index.

Carefully leveled text with a strong photo match offers early fluent readers the support they need to succeed.

Before Reading

- "Walk" through the book and point out the various nonfiction features. Ask the student what purpose each feature serves.
- Look at the glossary together. Read and discuss the words.

Read the Book

- Have the child read the book independently.
- Invite him or her to list questions that arise from reading.

After Reading

- Discuss the child's questions. Talk about how he or she might find answers to those questions.
- Prompt the child to think more. Ask: Tectonic plates formed many landforms on Earth, like mountains, gorges, and rifts. Have you ever seen a landform made by tectonic plates?

Pogo Books are published by Jump!
5357 Penn Avenue South
Minneapolis, MN 55419
www.jumplibrary.com

Copyright © 2021 Jump!
International copyright reserved in all countries. No part of this book may be reproduced in any form without written permission from the publisher.

Library of Congress Cataloging-in-Publication Data

Names: Gardner, Jane P., author.
Title: How tectonic plates shaped earth / Jane P. Gardner.
Description: Minneapolis, MN: Jump!, Inc., [2021]
Series: Earth shapers | Includes index.
Audience: Ages 7-10.
Identifiers: LCCN 2019028036 (print)
LCCN 2019028037 (ebook)
ISBN 9781645271260 (hardcover)
ISBN 9781645271277 (paperback)
ISBN 9781645271284 (ebook)
Subjects: LCSH: Plate tectonics—Juvenile literature. | Faults (Geology)—Juvenile literature. | Earth sciences—Juvenile literature. | Earth (Planet)—Internal structure—Juvenile literature.
Classification: LCC QE511.4 .G37 2021 (print)
LCC QE511.4 (ebook) | DDC 551.1/36—dc23
LC record available at https://lccn.loc.gov/2019028036
LC ebook record available at https://lccn.loc.gov/2019028037

Editor: Jenna Gleisner
Designer: Michelle Sonnek

Photo Credits: Photopictures/Shutterstock, cover; Alex Brylov/Shutterstock, 1; Malte Pott/Shutterstock, 3; Olga Danylenko/Shutterstock, 4; Oliver Denker/Shutterstock, 5; NYgraphic/Shutterstock, 6-7 (background); Peter Hermes Furian/Shutterstock, 6-7 (foreground); Andrea Danti/Shutterstock, 8-9; Alexander Izmaylov/Shutterstock, 10 (background); SharonFoelz/iStock, 10 (foreground); by wildestanimal/Getty, 11; Manuel Chinchilla/Shutterstock, 12-13; Dmitry Pichugin/Shutterstock, 14-15; Fotos593/Shutterstock, 16-17; Stocktrek Images/SuperStock, 18; MIKKEL JUUL JENSEN/Science Source, 19; Paruay Leelawong/Shutterstock, 20-21; Kenneth Dedeu/Shutterstock, 23.

Printed in the United States of America at Corporate Graphics in North Mankato, Minnesota.

TABLE OF CONTENTS

CHAPTER 1

SHAPING EARTH

Mount Everest is Earth's highest point. It is just over 29,000 feet (8,800 meters) tall! Moving tectonic plates formed it.

Mount Everest

Tectonic plates formed Earth's lowest spot, too! It is the Mariana **Trench**. It is almost 36,000 feet (11,000 m) below **sea level**.

trench

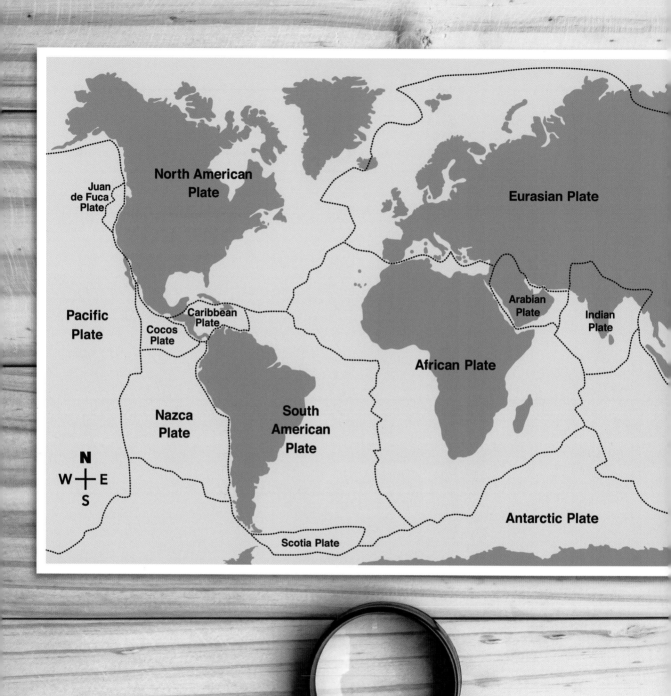

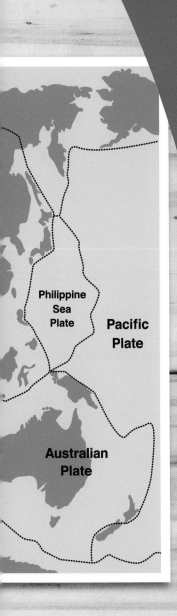

Tectonic plates are giant slabs of rock. They are pieces of Earth's **crust**. Scientists mapped them. Seven of them are bigger than continents! The Pacific Plate is the largest. It lies beneath the Pacific Ocean.

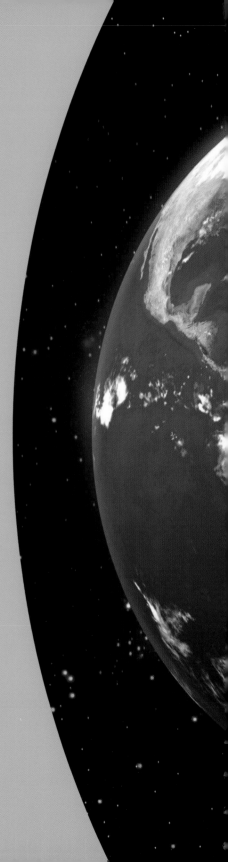

Heat moves the plates. How? Earth's **core** is very hot. It heats **magma**. The magma rises. It cools as it gets closer to the crust. Why? It is farther from Earth's core. The cooler magma sinks. Magma keeps heating and cooling. This moves the plates above it.

crust

mantle

outer core

inner core

CHAPTER 2

WAYS TO MOVE

Plates change Earth as they move. Landforms take shape where plates meet. These spots are boundaries. **Natural disasters** can happen, too. Like what? The motion of the ocean floor can cause **tsunamis**.

TSUNAMI
HAZARD
ZONE

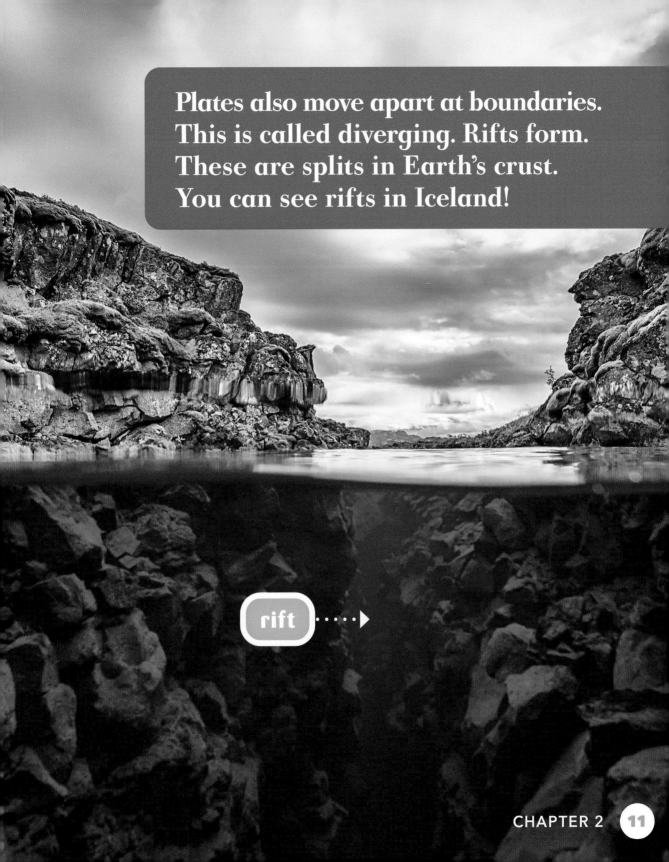

Plates also move apart at boundaries. This is called diverging. Rifts form. These are splits in Earth's crust. You can see rifts in Iceland!

rift · · · · ▶

Diverging plates also form **ridges** in the ocean. How? Plates move apart. Magma comes out of the split. It cools and builds up. This makes underwater mountains. The tops can form islands. The Bay Islands formed this way. They are in Honduras.

DID YOU KNOW?

Diverging plates make new ocean floor. The ocean gets larger!

Bay Islands

Andes
Mountains

Plates push together at some boundaries. This is called converging. Plates slowly crash together. Land is pushed up to form mountains.

One plate usually moves under the other. This is called **subduction**. Magma rises up. New mountains form. The Andes Mountains formed this way. Subduction forms ocean trenches, too.

DID YOU KNOW?

Volcanoes often form when plates converge. They form where they diverge, too! The Ring of Fire has many volcanoes. It surrounds the Pacific Ocean.

Plates also slide past each other. This is called transforming. **Friction** can stop them. **Pressure** builds up. It can release suddenly. This causes **earthquakes**! They can happen when plates converge, too.

TAKE A LOOK!

How do plates move at different boundaries? Take a look!

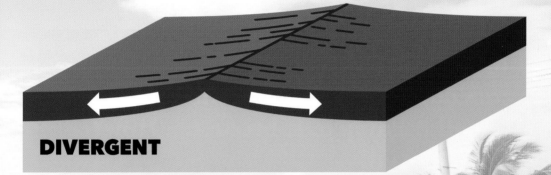

DIVERGENT

CONVERGENT

TRANSFORM

CHAPTER 3

ALWAYS MOVING

Earth looked very different millions of years ago. There was just one continent. We call it Pangea. It broke up. How? Plates moved!

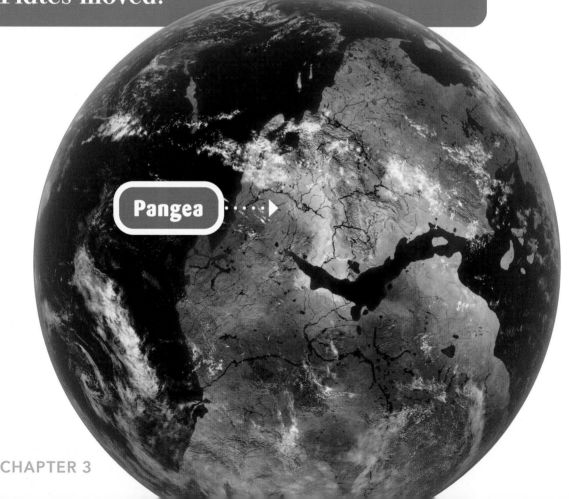

Pangea ·····▶

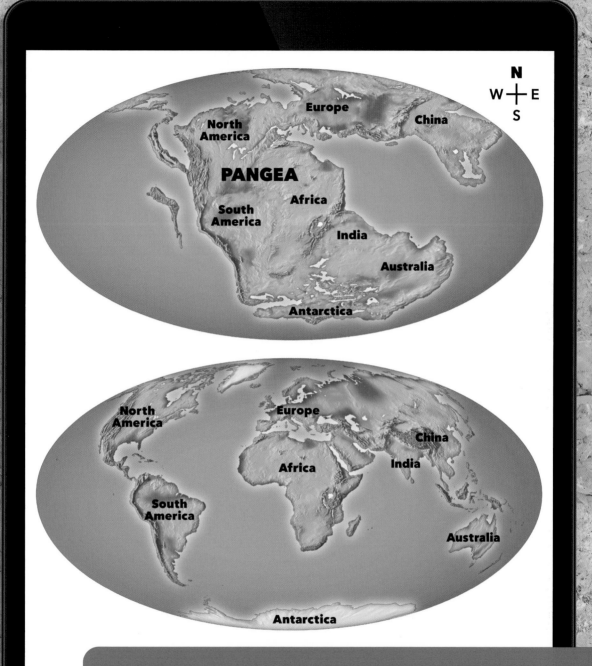

This is how the plates lie now. Can you see how they once fit together?

The plates are always moving. They move slowly, but they will continue to change Earth. Continents will shift.

Landforms will disappear. Others will form. How do you think Earth will change?

DID YOU KNOW?

How fast do plates move? Some move about one inch (2.5 centimeters) each year. Others move almost six inches (15 cm) each year!

ACTIVITIES & TOOLS

MAKE YOUR OWN TECTONIC PLATES

Plates move on a substance with a texture similar to pudding. Use pudding to see how plates move!

What You Need:
- packet of instant pudding mix
- 3 cups cold milk
- measuring cup
- mixing bowl
- spoon
- large, flat container
- graham crackers

1 Follow the directions on the instant pudding mix.

2 Pour the pudding into the container. Allow the pudding to set.

3 Break the graham crackers into large pieces. Place them on top of the pudding. Notice how they seem to "float" on the surface.

4 Gently move the graham crackers around. Try moving them like the different boundaries. What happens when they slide past one another? Does one push under another? How is this similar to tectonic plates?

5 Enjoy your tectonic plates snack!

GLOSSARY

core: The central part of Earth that is very hot.

crust: The hard outer layer of Earth.

earthquakes: Sudden shakings of the ground, often occurring where plates converge or transform.

friction: The force that slows down objects when they rub against each other.

magma: Melted rock beneath Earth's surface.

natural disasters: Sudden events in nature that cause serious damage or loss of life.

pressure: The force produced by pressing on something.

ridges: Long, narrow chains of mountains or hills.

sea level: The average level of the ocean's surface, used as a starting point from which to measure the height or depth of a place.

subduction: The action of one tectonic plate moving under another.

trench: A deep valley formed when one plate moves under another.

tsunamis: Very large, destructive waves caused by an underwater earthquake or volcano.

volcanoes: Mountains with openings through which molten lava, ash, and hot gases erupt.

INDEX

TO LEARN MORE

Finding more information is as easy as 1, 2, 3.

1. Go to www.factsurfer.com
2. Enter "howtectonicplatesshapedEarth" into the search box.
3. Choose your book to see a list of websites.

FACT SURFER